5 RULES
for
Drama-Free
Living

Elaine Bentley

Published by Elm Grove Press, LLC

To request information about our books, write to:
Elm Grove Press, LLC, P.O. Box 153, Old Mystic, CT 06372
Or visit us on the web at: www.elmgrovepress.org

Published 2017

ISBN: 978-1-940863-08-5

Cover and Interior Design: Walter Schwarz

Cover photo of Monument Peak, Montana
by Mary L. Cryan

Quotes used with permission:

Nikki Giovanni

Dave Grossman

Pema Chödrön Foundation

10 9 8 7 6 5 4 3 2 1

Printed in the United States of America

ELM GROVE

5 RULES
for Drama-Free Living

CONTENTS

If I have seen further than others,

it is by standing upon

the shoulders of giants.

—Isaac Newton

for Hap and Jerry,
Mom and Dad
—and The Lads, for all the Wahoo!

Homage and Acknowledgements

To my clients, for whom the initial essays were written: while I cannot list you by name, know that you will always have my gratitude for the opportunity to share the excavation and discover with you which of these concepts were worth keeping. I hope they will continue to be of use.

To all those teachers, researchers, therapists, theorists, and authors who have fed my hunger to understand and whose efforts have seeped so deeply into my thinking that discerning it from my own is sometimes tricky: please know that your gifts have fed many hungry spirits. For the wisdom of Gerry Arndt, Harry P. Dunne, Joe Esposito, Carolyn Scholz, Virginia Satir, Fritz Perls, Carl Whitaker, Bill O'Hanlon, John Bradshaw, David Burns, Kelly McGonigal, Wayne Dyer, Beth Jarman, Erich Fromm, Enid McIntosh Norris, Tom Fogarty, and the brilliant people at SMI, Nightingale Conant, Sounds True, Hay House, and CareerTrack: I am continually blessed by the miracle of your hard work. Please accept my apologies if I have failed to reference it sufficiently or to represent it fairly. All errors are my very own.

To all my honest readers and faithful cheerleaders, especially Elouise Bentley Hamilton Rector and Lynn Lenihan who faced those gritty first drafts with such gusto: high praise and profound gratitude. To Eva Carll-Albert, Jessica Meredith, Louisa K. Baker, Candy Leonard, Marilyn Venuti, Karen Marshall, and Karen Parker, and to those who read or listened to portions as they emerged, particularly Karen Ethier-Waring, Jude Rittenhouse, Platt Arnold, and Melanie Greenhouse: without your commitment of time, kindness, and compassionate critique my words would be far less readable.

To those who opened doors and did the heavy lifting in the publication process, special appreciation goes to David Arnold, Walter Schwarz at Figaro Design, and Ruth W. Crocker of Elm Grove Press. To say that I am fortunate to know you is a monumental understatement. You have my earnest thanks for your expertise, patience, and kindness. I really couldn't have done this without all of you.

Introduction

This book is about being awake to the power of attending to our selves as we make choices.

The mechanics of how we create patterns of thought and behavior, while widely known to the inner circle of psychotherapy professionals, are rarely shared in everyday language to the average intelligent consumer. This is my maiden effort to correct that omission–in a way that makes these ideas portable, memorable and, now and then, good for a laugh.

I decided I couldn't be everybody's therapist, so I assembled *5 Rules for* **Drama-Free** *Living* to get these powerful tools to the widest number of people for the greatest good.

The development of skills to connect with one's own truth and with our fellow beings is a basic journey of life. The way we manage stress (or crank up its volume) will help deepen emotional habits. When we make conscious choices instead of falling back into programs inherited from past generations—or absorbed unconsciously from the network of influences that surrounds us—we get to feel some power over our daily lives.

It is fairly old-school to take responsibility for one's own life and happiness, but it's a practice that has a very refreshing result: increased satisfaction coupled with significantly shorter times of real misery. Read on.

Practical Approach to the Rules

1. You get to choose. These ideas are really suggestions for new ways to look at your life–and your assumptions about it that may have been keeping you stuck. Only take them seriously if you are not already deeply satisfied with your life.

2. No perfection. Since we are human and ridiculously fallible, we can look to these rules as beacons for a more functional and satisfying way to live. If you aren't goofing some of the time, you probably aren't doing much. I love the AA slogans "Progress, Not Perfection" and "Practice Makes Progress".

3. You will forget. Periodically it is necessary to slap oneself on the forehead and say "I knew that!" We can only hold so much in our mind's ready files at once. Sometimes an old idea will arrive in new clothes as is the case with many here. Think of it as finding an old favorite shirt on the floor of your closet. Feel the comfort–and skip chastising yourself for letting it fall. Gravity happens.

4. It's hard. Well, yeah. If it were easy you'd have already done it. Changing patterns of thought and behavior takes time and effort. You may despair of breaking those habits as you, once again, watch your foot heading straight into your mouth. Just *noticing* the old pattern is progress. Check out Portia Nelson's famous poem just ahead.

5. Slow is good. When you try on new behaviors expect to be more successful with strangers and people who don't matter a lot to you. Much of what we do within our closest circle, with family, in particular, is done unconsciously. Plus they know where all your buttons are–they helped install them! Just know that as you set new routines of self care, responsibility, and assertiveness with strangers, acquaintances, and coworkers, it will gradually slip into your communications with friends and family as well.

6. Expect push-back. Not everyone will want you to change. Not that they don't love you and wish the absolute best for you–many do. But they too will have blind spots and stucknesses. Be patient with them and lovingly model the behaviors you'd wish them to learn.

7. Lead with compassion. Know that, as the Desiderata says, "Everyone has their story, even the dull and the ignorant." Treat others with empathy, without compromising your worth.

8. Resources abound. These are a mere reductive few. Take these and run with them. I promise you will trip over others (and when you do, record them for posterity).

9. You matter. Your feelings, ideas, and time matter. So do everyone else's. Take turns caring and being cared for, listening and allowing others to listen to you.

10. Be discerning. Not everyone deserves your opinion. Sometimes it's important to save your breath.

Autobiography in Five Short Chapters
by Portia Nelson

I
I walk down the street.
There is a deep hole in the sidewalk.
I fall in.
I am lost…I am helpless.
It isn't my fault.
It takes me forever to find a way out.

II
I walk down the same street.
There is a deep hole in the sidewalk.
I pretend I don't see it.
I fall in again.
I can't believe I am in the same place.
But it isn't my fault.
It still takes a long time to get out.

III
I walk down the same street.
There is a deep hole in the sidewalk.
I see it is there.
I still fall in…it's a habit.
My eyes are open.
I know where I am.
It is my fault.
I get out immediately.

IV
I walk down the same street.
There is a deep hole in the sidewalk.
I walk around it.

V
I walk down another street.

RULE ONE:

**There is one
and only one
thing in the world
that we have power over
and responsibility for–
and that is the person
in the mirror.**

Chapter One

ONE THING YOU CONTROL

"Darling," Javitz used to say,
"the first step toward enlightenment
is recognizing our own accountability."
—William J. Mann

There is one and only one thing in the world that I have power over. Myself. I am completely responsible for where I go with my feet, what I do with my hands, what I put in my body, what words come out of my mouth, and, most importantly of all, where I focus my mind.

I am responsible if I stay up too late to feel energetic in the morning, if I overspend, or if I blow off promises made to others.

I may not always control where my attention goes, but I can choose where my attention *stays*. I love the expression what one 'dwells on' because I imagine that as a literal place that one moves into, with pillow and teddy bear and blankie. The reality we bestow on ourselves (by our focus of attention) expands from a narrow set of examples (or one!) to become the perceived world, e.g. 'he turned away' becomes 'everyone hates me'.

Who we are becoming is more important than what we've been through. This is not to dismiss our suffering or our achievements but to say that those things that influenced our growth—however nourishing or harsh—were mere devices in the ultimate shaping of character. One of the dangers of poor-me thinking is that it interferes with a process in which we today hold the tools: the choice to live and to act in the now.

We humans have the power to make our own worlds on at least two fronts: first by manifesting through intention and concerted effort and, secondly, by focus, dwelling on chosen aspects of what we encounter and imagine. The final absolute freedom is choosing where we put our individual attention.

Driving provides a good example. When a car drifts into my lane, my *amygdala* (an organ that functions as the alarm bell in my brain's emotional zone) starts ringing out "OMG!" This cranks a burst of adrenalin into my body— faster than thought—to empower my rapid response to danger, in this case quickly turning the steering wheel to avoid collision (an automatic, almost involuntary result of having practiced driving for many years).

Then comes the voluntary portion of our show: thoughts. What do I tell myself about what just happened?

If I say, "Whew, that was a close call," dismiss what just happened and re-focus on the road in front of me, the *amygdala* gets the message to stand down, emergency over, no more adrenalin needed. My body can relax, with a big sigh, and go back to normal. "At ease."

Ah, but what if I have a particular peeve about that kind of vehicle or red cars remind me of my ex? I might tell myself that those people shouldn't be on the road, should be shot, there ought to be a law!

The *amygdala* gets the message that the danger is continuing, and it keeps sending its OMG message, triggering even more booster shots of stress chemicals (adrenalin, cortisol) into the body's systems to energize and sustain us for the coming battle with the saber-toothed SUV.

Can you see what might be problematic with this picture? I feel a little exhausted even imagining it. How much more so to actually live in this state day in, day out, as many do. Telling themselves that the world is SUCH a dangerous place that one must always be on Red- or at least Orange-Alert? So let's look at how we can use our own power in light of this process by turning to the breath.

Start with a sigh, a really big S- S- Si-i-i-i-i-igh. Ah-h-h-h-h. Breathing out all that overwhelm, all that it's-just-too-much-for-me energy. Don't worry about the in-breath, it will take care of itself. A full, deep sigh is in some ways a secret of a good life: It is the opposite of holding on to pain, to anguish, to resentment, to worry.

When I sigh, I let go of an imagined reality where I am in control of outcomes. I am only in control of and responsible for my *own* actions and attention.

There is a moment, a split second, at the bottom of the out-breath that is quiet. There is no in-breath needed just yet, only a still, sweet emptiness. Peace. No thought, just presence or perhaps Presence.

A moment of awareness without judgment or planning. A nanosecond of not-misery. A place so quiet and peaceful that you may find in it the space to hear something divine. Cosmic. True. Perhaps your own truth.

But more important perhaps is this tiny bit of time without effort or will. The bliss of giving up trying to manage the world can enter here. Stop trying. Allow the quiet, and, remarkably, answers start to arise. Resentments start to melt. Opportunities and options appear. Strategies become workable. *If-onlys* fade and *aha!s* brighten. So much can one discover there in the silence.

What you do with your mind and actions today, your very next decision, might even save the planet—or at least a bit of your own sanity.

Resisting the Now
We fantasize that with the right equipment, setting, or support system, we could do anything—write The Great American Novel, cure cancer, find Amelia Earhart. But without all that, *how?* Excuses of all sorts emerge. Not enough time. The bathroom wants cleaning. Not enough space on the desk. No desk.

But then there's someone like J K Rowling: a single mom on welfare writes a best-selling series of novels on napkins in a coffee shop. *Dang!* It's time to take myself seriously and be responsible for my own efforts.

Do you find yourself seeking distraction, something stimulating enough to divert attention away from whatever you are in the midst of? Stimulation enough indeed, to stir up biochemical activity in the brain about things that are *not even present*, not actually *real* in this moment, like anger at an old wound, or like a fidgety stomach about an upcoming date or meeting.

Is this because we really don't like to be present? Or might it be a mere habit of the mind, an artifact of a shared culture of *I can't wait* or of *if I hadn't*? So often heard as we grew up, we absorbed these habits of speech—and thus of thought—and made them the *normal* ways of our lives and minds. Still, let's not beat ourselves up about it—not useful! Let's do look at what else we can do.

The only time things can happen is in the Now.
Future things can be planned for, anticipated, dreaded. Past can be regretted or celebrated. Right Now is the only time when action is possible, even the actions of listing tasks to do in the Right Now of tomorrow, to writing letters of apology for something done in the Right Now of yesterday, or *moving one thing* of a huge project, the accomplishment of which exceeds the time boundaries of this moment.

Eckhart Tolle, bless his heart, has made a career telling us *The Power of Now*. OK, Ram Dass said it back in the 1970s, but obviously we still need remedial *Be Here Now* work.

One doesn't climb a mountain (or get a college degree) except by taking steps, literally or figuratively, in the Right Now.

Place the foot, shift the weight forward, lift the back foot, repeat a few thousand times, and you're at the top of the hill. Register for a class, buy the text, go to class, do the homework, go to class, do the research, write the paper, go to class, take the test. Show up, show up, show up. Repeat until you receive a diploma or degree. In each case, the action only occurs by taking responsibility in the Right Now.

Learn *not* to keep taking stuff on—and *to* make time-limited commitments. It's kind of a seasonal thing—more, more, more, then suddenly OMG! We get overcommitted.

Now when I feel a twinge of resistance, I check in with myself *Hmm, maybe I can skip this one meeting* or not volunteer *for this next task/board/project*. It may take a while to hone that skill, but in the long run, the discomfort I feel now helps me learn to pace myself *before* making those commitments. Remember, knowing your limits is NOT a failure; it's how you prevent same. End of sermonette.

> The attempt to avoid legitimate suffering
> lies at the root of all emotional illness.
> —M. Scott Peck

Sometimes, when a sense of vague unpleasantness arises, we hurry to distract ourselves rather than feel it. Sometimes, it may be important to do this. At other times, when the schedule allows or when the feeling reaches something we might be tempted to call misery, another approach may be called for: *To sit in and with* the sensation, without indulging in whatever stories that may come up.

7

Exercise: Learning to Listen to What Ails You
Observe the body's sensations without attaching meaning
or pressure to respond or to change.

Direct the mind only so much as to find this neutral
focus of attention, breathing slowly and deeply, and let
what ever shows up pass across your awareness and be
released, in a kind of mental out-gassing.

Avoid getting caught up in a story. To retell yourself
about the problems or concerns is to dwell in suffering.
This process is the opposite of struggle—it is surrender to
the sensation without labeling it *worry* or *anxiety* or *fear*
or *desolation,* rather to give in to the wash of feeling and to
stop struggling to block it. I liken it to flipping over on your
back rather than struggling to stay afloat in deep water.

At some point you may choose to write down an idea or a
task to be done later but return and *stay* with the attention
until the unpleasant energy has shifted into a sense of
peace, satisfaction, or practical focus which may arise.

By attending to the *sensation* and not the story we can
release the pain instead of reinvigorating the drama.
When we honor our feelings in this way, by receiving the
message, the body can release the need to keep sending
the misery signal. Then the mind can make clearer
decisions based on the well-being of the whole self.

RULE ONE:

and furthermore...

Chapter Two

STOP TRYING TO MANAGE THE WORLD

Never try to teach a pig to sing.
It won't work and it annoys the pig.
—Anonymous

Attempting to correct others—unless that is literally your job and sometimes even then—is mostly a waste of time. Even with those you *do* need to manage, your staff or minor children, the task is really to facilitate *their* self-management and autonomy. Coach when you must. Avoid micromanaging. It lowers the recipient's self esteem and triggers both resistance and resentment.

Quality control aside, we all need to crawl before we can walk.

"They are driving me crazy!"
We all know that feeling: Someone seems to be wearing out the path to your last nerve, to have the secret formula for poisoning any potential good time you might almost be having. *Why do they do that?*

A more useful question might be *how do I let them get to me?* Posing the question this way puts the power back in our own hands, allowing us to do something useful about it (assuming that the other person's behavior isn't illegal or immediately life-threatening*). Since the only person you have power over is yourself, then it's time to take responsibility for saving your own hide, calling in the Mounties when appropriate or getting the hell out of Dodge.

Let's talk about how you drive yourself crazy. "What?" you say. Why am I blaming you for what that other person or those other people are *doing to you?*

Actually, I'm not blaming you for their behavior—they are as responsible for their own choices as the rest of us. I'm actually holding up the mirror so you can catch the story you are using to trap yourself in others' lives (and business) instead of getting on with managing your own.

Dangers of Trying to Manage Others' Lives

- Overwhelm
- Others' resentment of the intrusion
- Frustration
- Emptiness and neediness because your *own* needs are not being met
- It just doesn't work

---

*In those cases, don't stop to finish this book. Call 911, a local domestic violence shelter, or consult an appropriate professional immediately. If no specific type of advisor comes to mind, call a counselor to help you sort out your priorities, being cautious to avoid advisers (like friends and family) who have their own vested interests in your decision. Check the Yellow Pages under social worker, counselor, psychotherapist, psychologist, or marriage and family therapist. You do remember the Yellow Pages, don't you? If not, there's always The Net. ;-) *Psychology Today* has a nice site.

If it's not given with an open heart—and no strings attached—it's not a gift, but a subtle form of coercion.

What about our desires to rescue each other— and our children—from pain and discomfort? Are we thereby distracting them from the very experience that would help them overcome suffering—learning to *surf* it, if you will.

Might we teach them to experience the 'owie', notice it, and let it float away? Obviously, there are exceptions that require stitches, etc. But overall, need we run to medicate our discomforts, with all those routines and substances available to us, or rather simply feel them for the moments they wash over us and then watch them wash away with the wave of the next thought, sensation, awareness?

The kind of relationship we have with ourselves will determine the kind of relationships we have with others. We tell others—including our children—how to treat us by the way we treat ourselves—and them. As we practice self-care, self-management, and self-awareness, we increase those nourishing qualities in the circles we travel.

> Whose Business Are You In? There are only three kinds
> of business in the universe: mine, yours, and God's.
> —Byron Katie

When the sun throws out solar flares, it's God's business. It only becomes *my* business if my cell provider's satellite function is disrupted and it drops my calls. When a celebrity's spouse is cheating, it's their business, not mine.

Exercise: Sit for a bit and pay attention to your thoughts.
Notice when your mind gets caught up in other people's business.

If you have not been invited to advise or share their load—or have not accepted this burden—None of My Business (NOMB) is a terrifically effective mantra.

When and where do I avoid facing Rule 1?
What does that get me?

RULE TWO:

We Are All Containers for Feelings

Chapter Three

CONTAINERS

Burying emotion exacts terrible consequences.
—Martha Grimes

Splinters

Whatever difficulties, pain, and trauma that we experience, and have not yet fully processed, go into the Container and wait. Stew. Ferment. Pressurize.

Sometimes we would rather not deal with old pain but would prefer to ignore it, like a splinter that would be uncomfortable to remove. We hope that it will dissolve or work its own way out. Sometimes we are right.

But all too often, the area around the splinter gets red and sore. It festers and painfully reminds us of what we've not yet faced and dealt with.

Without proper care, our Containers can leak, overflow, or explode—or the task of holding the contents in takes all our energy.

A lot of human effort and energy is spent keeping the lid on. When all your energy goes to this task, it starts to feel like there's a heavy weight on your chest. "Everything is just too hard."

At some point the effort to hold it all in becomes too much and we end up overflowing or exploding. We may start to leak, weeping for "no reason" or "over-reacting" because the present situation has elements that remind us subconsciously of prior unfinished processing. The leakages may come out in small evils and mean-spirited choices like cutting someone off in traffic or more passive kinds of aggression.

The care of the Container is three-fold when it comes to self-management—and the prevention of needless drama:

1. **Excavate**—make some space by clearing out old stuff you carry.

2. **Assert** yourself as you go—stop stuffing what could be handled, with a little finesse, now.

3. **Strengthen** the Container—treat yourself like the precious, vulnerable, and resilient human that you are so you can hold what you need to.

EXCAVATE the contents of the Container. Dump it out. Sort and categorize them so you can choose what to digest or compost. Then fumigate. This makes room for the normal stresses and strains of life—and for those unforeseeable crises that sometimes overwhelm us.

Strategies for Excavating your Container:

Lists
Strategically, a list is like an extension of your brain. It's an extra hard drive that's available at times when your processer may be too challenged to work effectively. By making a list on the *outside* of body and mind, you don't

have to carry it all *inside*. Additionally, it offers specific targets for next steps—especially when it's used to sort priorities or to look at which things you *do* have some control over from those you may simply need to let go.

Writing a list when someone has ticked you off (pushed one of your buttons) helps do several things:

- Takes some of the heat out of communication to protect relationships from overstatement, backlash, and what a client once called *pissitivity*
- Takes the stress out of your body and puts it on paper
- Once the list cools, it allows you, without drama, to examine the contents for facts and validity, for relevance, and for consideration of whether they need further processing, either alone or with another person

When something becomes difficult to handle, lists can help the brain work more effectively. They can give you some perspective and the opportunity to treat yourself as kindly as you might treat a good friend in a similar spot.

Lists may include these written conversations with self:
What do I feel right now?
What are my thoughts?
Can I tell my opinions from facts?
How do my judgments or assumptions color my thinking process?

With two conflicting choices, make two lists (pros/cons or Choice A/B) to flesh out what is going on inside you—to make a more thoughtful decision.

Journaling

A journal is like having a therapist in your back pocket. It's always there to listen, affirm, and clarify. Writing to your future self can take you out of feeling stuck and into the satisfaction of having clarity—or even a plan.

Journaling is longitudinal, a conversation with oneself over a span of time. Reading our own past writings, we become aware of how we look at things now versus then. We can notice patterns.

My journal always travels with me. In those times *between:* on airplanes, in waiting rooms, when stranded, or unexpectedly alone, I find the most magical things get written. Perhaps this happens because I have stepped out of my scheduled life. A journal makes me feel real, especially when I have moved on or relationships have ended and faded. I am able to visit another me who has spoken intimately, thoughtfully, bearing witness to the world's changes, to maturity, and with humility, to the biggest, broadest goofs—also known as FGOs (Freaking Growth Opportunities)—ever made.

Letters Not to Send

Contrast that journal conversation-with-self with the necessary-to-survival writing I call (apologies to my sister for the language here) the "Dear Asshole Letter", one written and NEVER to be sent.

These can also be written into one's journal if privacy is assured. This is pedal-to-the-metal writing that shrugs off editing like unwelcome hangers-on, gives voice to unspoken rage, long-buried, silenced by decorum, and by the desire to hurt no one's feelings. The D.A.L. has these guidelines: no-stopping, no rules, no mercy. D.A.L.s help me discover core truths that my polite self would not have dared to say. If I had thought these would be read I would have edited myself, slammed on the brakes and lost momentum, stuck myself between needing release and needing approval.

The D.A.L. allows no apologies. It purges. It scrapes the sides of the compost bin, enriching, nourishing my growth, despite myself. Later, when things have cooled and clarified, there may come a letter that *can* be sent.

Written Dialogues
These allow us to have conversations with different aspects of ourselves.

One exercise uses the non-dominant hand to write feeling questions and concerns, and then the dominant-hand writes a response from the thinking self. This technique can loosen knots that have been surprisingly tough to undo.

The value of dumping troubling thoughts and uncomfortable emotions onto paper, where we come back to them later, is inestimable. Writing releases the physiological side effects of holding back, gives us clarity, and helps avoid the guilt of dumping on others. It offers the thinking mind a chance to dialog with the feeling mind. So often, head overcomes heart without vital understanding, or heart overruns head in the stampede of unbridled passion. The left-brain/right-brain conversation in the journaling process can get us closer to what Marsha Linehan (1993) calls Wise Mind—"that part of each person that can know and experience truth."

ASSERT yourself. Express your preferences instead of putting new stuff into the Container. Acting out anger (or other emotions) is radically different from being in touch with the feeling. Many people never learn the difference. There are times when feelings must be stored until a later time because there's a higher priority in that moment (like saving a child's life or keeping one's job). And saying we don't like or want something is not the same as throwing a hissy fit about it.

Outside of emergencies, deal with situations and feelings directly as they come up so that the backlog of unspoken thoughts and feelings doesn't come around to bite you and those around you in the butt. At the same time, avoid biting off people's heads which just puts more stuff in *their* Containers, which will likely to come *back at you* sooner or later. Not useful or fun.

Say what you mean. Mean what you say. Don't say it mean. Learn to say the simple truth in appropriate ways, with loving-kindness. Assertiveness is not aggression (which would trigger a fight-back response from others), but an I'm-here-and-I-choose-to-have-a-voice message: please don't steamroll over me.

STRENGTHEN the Container so it can hold what it needs to for short-run emergencies, whether we're talking about flat tires or the zombie apocalypse. *The body itself is the Container.* No one else can care for your Container but you.

From the inside out:
W. Robert Nay (2010) suggests we pay attention to
The 5 Ss: "Sleep, Stress, Substances, Sustenance, and
Sickness." Good *physical* self-care includes nutrition,
"sleep hygiene", and reasonable exercise. ("Sleep
hygiene" is the sum of the habits and practices that are
conducive to sleeping well.)

Bodywork like massage or yoga, acupuncture, and
routine health screenings apply here. According
to the Uplefgdger Instittute, your body's *fascia*—
the bands of fibrous connective tissue enveloping,
separating, and binding together muscles, organs,
and other soft structures of the body —holds
emotion. *S-t-r-e-t-c-h several times a day for mood
management, mental and physical refreshment,
and inner awareness.*

Note that sugar and caffeine can put your body on an
emotional rollercoaster. Sufficient protein early in the
day for stable blood sugar can go a long way towards
keeping you out of therapy or divorce court. To that
end, a personal rule I try to follow is *Breakfast like a
king, lunch like a prince, and dinner like a pauper.*

From the outside in:
Spiritual or *energetic* self-care is about paying
attention to activities that feed your sense of well-
being. Whether going to church or standing by a river
with a fishing pole in your hand. Or rolling on the
floor with a big fluffy dog or laughing with a small
child. Losing yourself in creativity: gardening, knitting

or song. Witnessing a sunrise or hearing a great piece of music. The key is deep involvement in something that takes your consciousness out of the angst, out of the concerns of managing the world and/or *into* a sense of flow or replenishment, connection with something greater than the minutiae of your daily concerns.

Movies and books can give this relief sometimes, but do watch out for books or shows with suspense that can *increase* the stress you carry. The rapid heart rate, the edge-of-the-seat feeling are evidence that the body believes there is some real threat which *adds* stress to the Container.

Learn to Love Your Triggers
We all have them, the buttons on the outside of the Container that turn loose that shit-storm on unsuspecting friends, family, coworkers, innocent bystanders—and ourselves.

Find a way to be grateful for the information in your frustration. Use the energy released by your annoyance to capture those feelings onto paper. Let 'em cool, and then go back when you have time and privacy and give that frustrated kid inside you a good listening to.

Need Heavy Equipment to Do that Excavation?
There are times when each of us needs an outside specialist to help with that process. When relationships crumble or overwhelm is setting in, having a professional listener is one useful strategy.

If you have survived "Big T" Trauma (or chronic small-t trauma), go for a therapist who is Certified in Eye-Movement Desensitization and Reprocessing (EMDR), a treatment that uses Adaptive Information Processing, the heavy equipment earthmover of the counseling world. Best known for its remarkable application in many cases of Post-Traumatic Stress Disorder (PTSD), EMDR helps the brain cool down some of the over-stimulated emotional patterns and helps it function more normally. That same ability is what defuses the smaller everyday traumas of normal human life.

Check EMDRIA's website to find a Certified EMDR therapist.
http://www.emdria.org/search/custom.asp?id=2337

Exercise: Sleep Is My Friend
Quality sleep is critical for strengthening the Container. Without it, not much goes well. Often, worry thoughts or merely a rehash of the day's stimulating or stressful activities can get in the way of the relaxation we need to get to sleep.

Focus gently on a neutral image and you leave no room for troubling thoughts.

Here's a method I use that helps me get to sleep easily:

In your mind's eye, imagine a soft rectangle on its side whose corners are, without strain, at the far extent of your vision.

*Starting at any one corner, envision the number **100**. Then moving to the next corner, see a **99**,*

*continuing along picture a **98**,*

and so on, corner to corner and around the rectangle until sleep takes you.

The slight effort needed to *envision* the numerals, combined with the mild stimulation of the visual cortex, seems to shift us effectively out of both past and future thoughts, and thus facilitates slipping easily into rest.

(Sometimes after a dozen or so numbers, I will shift directions. That is, after a few leisurely laps around clockwise, I'll switch to counter-clockwise—or vice versa—preferring to balance the slight muscle effort by not always moving in the same direction.)

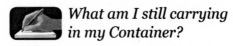 *What am I still carrying in my Container?*

_____

_____

_____

_____

_____

_____

_____

_____

_____

_____

_____

_____

_____

_____

_____

_____

_____

_____

_____

RULE THREE:

Feelings
Do Not
Mature

Chapter Four

EMOTIONS DO NOT MATURE

When you were born you were totally aware that there
is absolutely nothing wrong with you.

And then you got older. And things happened.
And you started to forget the Truth.

You started moving out of the awareness of love
and into fear, doubt, and judgment.

—Christine Hassler

Thinker/Feeler

We are born—as little tiny beings—already fully loaded
with the programs for *feelings*, relating to the world by
way of our bodily sensations. *This does not mature.*

What *does* mature is insight and the capacity to manage
ourselves when we have those feelings. What *does*
change is our *relationship to the experience* of our
feelings: we change the way we contain them as we
grow up, altering the stories we tell ourselves about the
information that we perceive through our emotions,
the intensity, weight, and value we give them. We gain
maturity in the way we express ourselves and in our
ability to choose a time and place more likely to allow
us to be successful in getting heard.

"Parts Is Parts"[1]

From Freud through Transactional Analysis to Internal Family Systems, people have talked about parts of the personality. Now we know that much about those qualities can correlate to parts of the human brain. Different parts of the brain have different attributes and develop over different periods of the lifespan, and the personality undergoes changes as that happens.

We all utilize different facets of ourselves at different times. There's a saying that one's emotional age is inversely proportional to the distance to one's parental home, or the closer I get to my parents, the less mature I feel—a visceral reminder that our internal experiences shift, automatically and unconsciously, as does the way we respond to others.

I'm all about keeping it simple, so I focus (primarily and simplistically) on two aspects: The Thinker and the Feeler.

Don't think that this Thinker vs. Feeler stuff is hierarchical.

These two aspects of self have different qualities, skill sets. The Feeler is found primaliry in the more central *deep limbic system* of the brain. The Feeler is rather like a precocious 3 year old who has very clear preferences, wants her ice cream *now,* has no filters—or boundaries generally—and lives in the present moment without concern or the capacity to plan for the future.

The Thinker's executive function activity takes place in the *frontal cortex,* the area behind your forehead. It is one-step removed from the flavors of the present moment and considers whether there's enough ice cream to go around or if the cholesterol content needs to be taken into account before having a second bowl. The Thinker—or Inner Adult—has the ability to assess cause and effect and to make long-term logistical considerations.

Both parts have importance if we are to have satisfying lives. We get into trouble when one really dominates and the other is ignored. Imagine someone whose Thinker runs the show without consideration for his own Feeler. They make decisions based on what is "best" according to purely logical standards, for example, choosing a career based exclusively on how much can be earned rather than how intrinsically satisfying the work might be.

And when someone's Feeler is in charge? Think of those people who are high-demand, moody, passionate, and high drama, rich material for an artist perhaps. Without the Thinker's skill at nose-to-the-grindstone persistence, the quantity or quality of actual work produced can tend to be spotty. Put the kid in charge of your relationships? Lots of bridges may be burned. And be sure not to leave the Feeler in charge of the credit cards or the car keys, especially if you live near a casino.

On the other hand, think of how that joyful Inner Child brings a zest to the hardworking Thinker's life—and how the, perhaps stoic, Adult can create a safe and sustainable place for the Child to play. When these two aspects of self operate from mutual trust and consideration, the whole self experiences an enhanced quality of life, *joie de vivre*, and reduced morning-after regrets.

The Inner Child

The Feeler, in the older and more primitive parts of the brain, is sometimes called The Inner Child, a concept popularized by Charles Whitfield (1987). The Feeler has aspects of both the *Free Child* and the *Adapted Child*.

THE FREE CHILD is the most honest and naive part of the Feeler, natural, unboundaried, unfiltered, unselfconscious, all about me (healthy narcissism). He can be loud and demanding or delightful and sweet. "I want what I want when I want it". Emotions can change quickly without residue (pleasure to dismay, love to rage).

When we are small—and the Thinker (frontal cortex) is still developing—we learn many things and create grooves or patterns (neural pathways) by the repetition of behaviors and experiences. In the early years, the unfiltered Feeler (Free Child) receives a lot of feedback about what not to do, in response to poorly executed or *verboten* behavior, mistakes we make due to having *just arrived on the planet.*

THE ADAPTED CHILD
Gradually, throughout childhood, another layer of the self comes into being as a kind of defense, an armor of sorts built of our memories of and responses to the many rules and negations that the Free Child encounters. Harsh touch and painful experiences train us that it can be unsafe to reach out to others.

The Adapted Child, a *Pseudo*-Adult self, is the most reactive part of the Feeler. She sometimes may even be *parentified*, given tasks and responsibilities beyond her age, may hold onto patterns of imperious, bossy, or condescending actions, while feeling fragile inside, and try to avoid overwhelm at all costs. Healthy narcissism is replaced by deceptive self interest. External appearance and internal have-to thinking or a "gotta-gotta" gerbil-on-the-wheel mindset can help form patterns that trouble our lives for years.

The *Pseudo*-Adult alter ego has learned to filter its speech (and stuff the Container) so as not to be criticized or hurt others' feelings. It often has learned to feel ashamed of its previous free and unbridled behavior. It may be burdened with a heavy layer of guilt and a sense of inadequacy born of experiencing the natural and age-appropriate ineptness of being a child. This part holds our rigid boundaries and shame-based language and thoughts. It may have learned to externalize these feelings and measure others by a similar, unfair standard, becoming at times judgmental or bullying. It spreads "shoulds" around like confetti and streamers.

THE ADULT, the Thinker, the cognitive brain, executive function, "good inner parent", can manage semi-permeable boundaries, understands cause and effect, has the power to communicate with and integrate all the parts. The Adult self is evidenced in modulated level tone of voice with reasonable and *controlled* volume and clarity.

The Thinker relates specifically to the later-developing prefrontal area of the brain which has responsibility for motivation, management, and planning. It can pay attention to the Feeler and use that information to make mindful choices and actions. Most of us need practice to strengthen the automatic *mature* responses to stress because we still have those 'grooves' that were installed by experience when we were small.

It is the *Pseudo*-Adult we wear as our identity until our brain has grown enough for us to individuate from the standards others impose on us. We may even believe it is who we really are. Sometimes, even long after we're grown, we don't quite believe in our own adulthood and don't feel the natural authority we have over ourselves.

We believe we are fake grownups, like we are pretending. We may come across as pompous or authoritarian. We extort our wants and needs from others—even those we love—by ramping up the drama. The reactive "drama queen" (or king) is operating from this less-skilled *Pseudo*-Adult whose voice may range in an instant from whiny or petulant to loud and demanding.

Or we may live in a kind of perpetual apology—bending over backwards in hopes of eventual acceptance, absolution, exoneration. The tendency toward white lies to avoid conflict, to be passive-aggressive, aggressively self-protective or passively powerless, and to hold on to negative experiences, grudges, and feelings resides in this trying-its-damnedest-to-seem-adult part of the self. Its tunnel vision, focused on appearing good-enough, works to get us grown. But it may fail dramatically when it comes to getting us a satisfying life or partner.

Don't bend over backwards;
people don't appreciate it, and it hurts your back.
—*anonymous*

Small Magics

My little self hears
difference of perspective
as criticism, rejection.

I want to tell her "it's ok"
but she holds this sadness
like a used lollipop,

linted in travel,
caught in a dizzy-colored
sticky swirl.

My little self
is stubborn, clings
to familiar struggles,

as if by repetition
she might learn the rhyme
and break their spell.

—EBB

Now I See It→What Can I Do?

Manage how you express and experience intensity–
don't let it manage you. Honor the Feeler in all its faces.
However awkwardly, it got you grown. Give that creative
little bugger its due. If you look down on yourself for past
errors, you waste NOW energy.

The worst part of your behavior is not who you are. The
Adult in you has the capacity to love and accept the Child,
as is, while gently and consistently directing it toward
constructive and compassionate choices. Without that
stewardship, the Child's anxiety and lack of self-trust will
trigger the limbic-hijack that looks to the world like a
meltdown or a brat attack.

Picture your younger, fragile self. Imagine that child
sitting next to you on the sofa. Can you let it lean over
against you? Will it let the Adult-you put your arm
around it? There's no hurry.

Building trust takes time, especially if there's a history
of self-shaming and a sense of not being acceptable. Let
the connection grow gradually. Become companions with
a two-way give-and-take, like a good big brother/little
brother relationship. Eventually, it may allow you to take
it into your heart.

Everyone needs empathy. We want to be seen, heard, and
valued. To have our ideas and experiences appreciated
and understood. To be treated fairly. The experience of
receiving empathy facilitates clear thinking, allows the
Feeler-mind to cool off, and lets the most adult part of the
brain operate without limbic interference.

35

The Importance of Wahoo!
One online discussion of a recent Tom Robbins'
novel talks about Wahoo this way: *that mysteriously
generated concentrate of exhilaration...sometimes
referred to as "syrup of wahoo", a kind of emotional
extract produced by the simultaneous boiling down of
beauty, risk, wildness, and mirth.*

One big part of taking good care of our Containers is
the experience of simple joy-in-the-moment. Laughing
aloud, singing with the band or the radio, dancing,
being intellectually stimulated, having a delightful sex
life, breathing the ocean's mist, basking in the light.
Remember that the Wahoo factor is wonderful for stress
relief and mood management.

The Importance of Mourning as Self-Care
I was once told that one should go to at least one funeral
per year. Even if you don't know the person, the presence
of others in mourning will tap into your reservoir of loss
and help you release some of it from your Container.

You may be crying for the person who has died, for
those closest, or those merely touched by them—or your
tears may be for your own burdens. The opportunity to
tap deeply into that well and just let it flow allows your
authentic pain to be released naturally, without engaging
in drama.

While it may leave you feeling wrung out for the
moment, a good sleep and some cold teabags on your
eyes in the morning, and you'll start the next day a little
bit lighter.

On Suffering

Looking at the suffering of innocents, as well as that of those of us who are less than innocent, one wonders "Why?" I've come to believe that life is a school and the question becomes not "how much do you suffer?" but "what do you do with the pain?"

If life is a school, pain is a textbook. From this we may read the lessons and learn, if we so choose, to polish ourselves on the abrasive skin of the world. The alternative is fear, closing against the pain, refusing to come to knowledge, to understanding, to wisdom.

Contrary to old belief, suffering is not noble. Avoiding discomfort is natural, healthy, *sane* even. But once it *is* visited upon us, it seems best to open to it. Welcome it, feel it thoroughly, and lighten the heart, in knowledge of powerlessness, riding upon the waves of pain and sadness, as if surfing, awaiting the lesson.

The closing-down process—trying to avoid the inevitable— like tensing in a car accident, may well injure one further. On the other hand, a relaxed approach may somehow cushion the blow, as it might for a drunken or sleeping person, the body's natural flexibility and resilience adapting to sudden impact. A ton of bricks is still a ton of bricks, but there's no sense butting it with your head.

Feeling Batty?

When old feelings arise, we become fearful. We fear that being present with those hidden, stored or half-forgotten memories might put us terribly at risk of going off the deep end.

One evening, I discovered a bat flying around in my bedroom. Needless to say, it was not a calming experience. The part of me that wanted to sleep clung, for a bit, to denial. ("It'll be okay, probably find its own way out. I don't have to do anything.") After it flew over my bed a few more times, I thought to open the trap door to the attic so it could go back up there and stay out of *my* space.

Finally, I decided to open a window upstairs, to offer this dark entity a clear path out into the open so both it and I could be released from the trauma of our encounter.

Later, as I sat with a client who was struggling to tell a story she found shameful, I thought of that poor terrified creature, struggling to escape. I told her the story of the bat which, like her secret, was distressingly disruptive while trapped inside.

Perhaps it is time to open a window in the heart.

If you feel like you are gonna blow, BLOW!
You know those times when you are full of feelings and can't think straight? It is *not* a personal failing like you may have been led to believe. This is the science behind why that happens.

Research via brain scan shows that when emotions are activated–let's say by an argument–the limbic system tends to monopolize the glucose metabolism (brain juice) and starves out the Thinker for a while. In PTSD, this condition can become chronic.

It is a biological condition which takes a minimum of SIX SECONDS to offset. Doesn't sound like very long, does it? It really isn't.

Imagine THREE N-I-C-E, L-O-N-G, S-L-O-W, D-E-E-P BREATHS. That takes about 6 seconds. In fact, it's one of the very best ways to get back into your Thinker brain after an upset. Here are a couple of reasons why:

1. When you tell yourself that there's a crisis you *activate the Feeler Brain* and take the Thinker off-line. By concentrating on the breath, you stop that process at the source.

2. Breathing is one of the few body processes that can operate both consciously/voluntarily and unconsciously/involuntarily. Taking over the conscious pacing of the breath serves as a device for managing the unconscious symptoms of distress like heart rate.

Exercise: The Blow Breath
Generally, people say "take a deep breath" to calm down, but if the lungs are halfway full, it's difficult to breath in deeply. So I like to start a deep breath with an out-breath first.

By beginning with a hearty expulsion of breath, like you'd use to blow out birthday candles, you make room for that N-I-C-E, S-L-O-W, D-E-E-P inhale. A tiny pause at the top and bottom of each breath adds even more calming.

Practice three of these breaths, three times a day, for three weeks. ("21 days to make or break a habit."[2]) You'll find that you start to shift to the out-breath habitually when you feel stressed.

Also, practice the Blow Breath consciously when you need to do things that are difficult. From carrying heavy laundry upstairs, to waiting in long lines, to dealing with traffic, children, telemarketers, or even a difficult bowel movement. Using a self-care (and mind-management) device like this for the smaller routine stresses of life makes the skill stronger and more automatically available for the bigger challenges.

Chapter Five

INTERMISSION
Evolving the Rules

Rule One—It's on each of us as individuals to choose how to apply our energies and attention, to take responsibility for our own choices and actions, and to avoid taking over for others.

Rule Two—Our Containers can hold only so much. When we clear out any stress backlog, practice self-care and assertive communication, we can maintain our resilience.

Rule Three—Our Adult/Thinker parts and our Child/Feeler parts balance well when we use them mindfully and give correct tasks to each part. Communication between these inner parts helps maximize present-moment joy and minimize I-wish-I'd-done-it-differently regret.

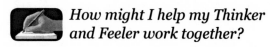 *How might I help my Thinker and Feeler work together?*

RULE FOUR:

What We Practice We Become

Chapter Six

PRACTICE → BECOME

The mind is everything,
what you think, you become.
–Buddha

We are what we repeatedly do.
Excellence, then, is not an act, but a habit.
—Aristotle

"I Just Wanna Be Happy. Is that so much to ask?"
Many times clients sit in my office and utter those words,
desperate for respite from their misery. I am inspired to
smile inside at the irony of the juxtaposition of *just*, in
this context a minimizing word, like asking for a sliver
of cake, "just a bit", and *happy*, a condition so vaguely
defined that it's like heading for Sacramento knowing
only that it is someplace out west.

So I try to help people define what happiness would
be *for them*. Of course, that requires that I look hard
at how I conceptualize it for myself. I came up with the
following as a working model. See what you think.

I believe that **happiness has two main components**:
pleasure (or joy-in-the-moment) and contentment.

Joy, like that wonderful new-baby-hit-the-jackpot-got-
the-promotion-first-real-spring-day-glorious-rock-rift
moment, is like a perfect pearl that shines in every

direction, past and future as well as present. We can look ahead to a summer day's outing with anticipatory joy. We can bask in the afterglow of a wonderful night at a concert.

Contentment is more like the thread on which we string those pearls. It lasts longer and is less showy, but is a consistent *living from one's values* which holds those treasured moments together. It can include contribution to the quality of life on the planet or in one's neighborhood: day-to-day being the kind of person who is okay to see in the mirror. Contentment also means being free from torture: not having a job that creates a living-for-the-weekend lifestyle or a relationship you dread going home to. Not being hungry or afraid all the time or in great pain. Being mostly alright, good enough, much of the time.

The combination of this thread and these pearls—this strand—is what I call happiness. Without the thread— and the knots that provide some spacing—there is chaos with periodic bright spots. Nothing to connect the moments of pleasure, no coherence, but a kind of pinball movement from shiny thing to shiny thing, no trust that there will ever be another peak moment. Without the pearls, contentment could be dull, somewhat colorless, untextured.

This theory is still new. I may tweak it some yet, but today, I'm happy with it.

How to build that *strand*?
Practice. Make your neural pathways work for you.

We get really good at what we practice. By consciously focusing the Thinker on tasks to be done—instead of on what we or others did poorly in the past—we develop a capacity for doing that chosen thing later on and with more ease. Compare this with the lost time and energy spent on regrets, dread, or fault-finding. It's not only hard to move forward while constantly looking backward—it's positively dangerous.

Researchers say that 'neurons that fire together, wire together'. The more often a pathway is used, with focus on positive feelings and goals, the stronger and better established those patterns get and the longer they last.

These pathways become a road map of our behavior, including automatic thoughts and routine responses. If not stimulated (used), these paths die off.

What does all of this mean to those of us who aren't brain surgeons?
When you unplug from pattern, it eventually dissipates. The pattern has no inherent life of its own beyond that which is animated by use.

Our experiences of danger or trauma in the past may create or energize pathways of reaction that get activated in the present. Responses triggered are out of proportion with the immediate situation. Just think what feelings arise for you when your boss says "Come into my office." If you get a sensation of being in the 6th grade and getting called to the Principal's office, you know *exactly* what I'm talking about. We animate crisis patterns when we get hooked by drama. Increased arousal of our reactive and survival patterns makes for decreased resilience in terms of what the Container can hold. "Under stress, we regress."

It Takes Time for Your Car to Know Its Way Home

New drivers have higher car insurance rates. They have not yet had time–practice–dodging squirrels, potholes, and other road hazards so that *a safe maneuver becomes automatic*, that is, from a sub-cortical neural network developed over time and experience.

Initially, driving takes effort and extremely focused attention. Once that neural pathway is built–that 'groove' or 'rut' is made–we may at times arrive at our destinations with no memory of the drive itself. Likewise, if one is used to driving a standard transmission car and switches to an automatic, the left foot will continue for some time to reach for a non-existent clutch pedal. Or if one is accustomed to an automatic transmission and changes to a standard, one will stall out frequently until that tricky clutch-brake-accelerator program is fully developed.

Are You Practicing What You *Really* Want to Do?

Lieutenant Colonel David Grossman[3] has written and teaches extensively on managing the mind. He tells this story on his website:

> One police officer gave another example of learning to do the wrong thing. He took it upon himself to practice disarming an attacker. At every opportunity, he would have his wife, a friend or a partner hold

a pistol on him so he could practice snatching it away. He would snatch the gun, hand it back and repeat several more times. One day he and his partner responded to an unwanted man in a convenience store. He went down one aisle, while his partner went down another. At the end of the first aisle, he was taken by surprise when the suspect stepped around the corner and pointed a revolver at him. In the blink of an eye, the officer snatched the gun away, shocking the gunman with his speed and finesse. No doubt this criminal was surprised and confused even more when the officer handed the gun right back to him, just as he had practiced hundreds of times before. Fortunately for this officer, his partner came around the corner and shot the subject.

A repeated conscious behavior becomes an unconscious habit.

Habits of Thought Create Patterns in the Brain
Imagine what happens when you practice:

- satisfaction/gratitude vs. self-recrimination and blame
- equanimity via meditation vs. fault-finding
- mindfulness (by choosing, over and over again, to slow down and pay attention) vs. gossip

MINDFULNESS: The Art of Noticing
What does it take to be mindful? The *capacity to resist*
or to *simply notice* the many distracters generated by
the mind (that can seduce one's focus causing it to flit
around) and the *internal authority* to repeatedly return
to the preferred point of attention. (I think there were
at least seven of these tempters that sparked in my brain
while I wrote that last sentence, including the temperature
of the room, a thought about lunch, a mild headache, and
some self-questioning about which words to put in or
leave out.)

Some distractions might be recollections of activities
begun yesterday and left unfinished. Some are nagging
physical sensations. Some could be triggered by the
ominous alarm clock or the party next door. Some are
creative considerations—and the many roadblocks to their
execution.

Pema Chödrön (1997) says, in her audio book *Don't Bite
the Hook*, that we can simply look at our experiences as
pleasant, unpleasant, or *neutral,* rather than getting
ourselves in a blither, either positive or negative.
Just note "pleasant" with a little internal mini-
celebration, a Buddha smile of contentment. This can
be done multiple times a day. Name "unpleasant" the
experiences that might otherwise trigger stronger and
more anguish-filled reactions, then release them by
moving the attention to see what pleasant conditions
one might notice. Maybe it is a strange idea, but it
merits exploration as one way to avoid getting on what I
call the "Drama Train."

When I make conscious decisions with awareness, versus floating into circumstances or ruts, I am exercising my power over those aspects of my life that *are* within my control: where I go with my feet, what I do with my hands, what I put in my body, what words come out of my mouth, and, most importantly of all, where I put my attention.

Meditation is a mindfulness practice that will soothe the parts of the brain that keep you wanting to always go, go, go. A regular meditation practice can result in lower blood pressure, decreased cravings for nicotine and alcohol, better concentration at work and in school, and improved communication by activating and energizing the patterns for calm and clarity.

Benefits of meditation suggested by research and experience[4]:

- Better digestion
- Reduce TMJ (Temporal Mandibular Joint) symptoms
- Lower Blood Pressure
- Clearer thinking
- Improved creativity
- More organized life
- Reduce Attention Deficit symptoms
- Less reactive
- Episodes of bliss

Simple but not easy. Because minds are like toddlers, easily distracted, we will need to repeat this gentle redirection–some seven times per sentence maybe–while training the mind to stay on task–building those new neural grooves. The elders in the world of meditation call it "practice" for just that reason.

Sample that space as much as possible, until it feels like home, as practice for routine calm and as jamming device against negative thought. If you've ever plugged your ears and sung "lalalalalalalala" against the onslaught of unwelcome input, you know the advantage of this: negativity can roll right on without affecting you.

A special note: some people who have a lot of worry thoughts and a great deal of anxiety may despair of meditation because they believe they cannot do it. The thing to recall here is that everyone does this automatically, but we tend to zone in on hyper-stimulating things like TV or worst-case-scenario stories. For anxiety of this sort, use a more active type of meditation called 'guided imagery.' (Check out Belleruth Naparstek's CDs for some good examples.) Or focus the mind consciously and repeatedly on loving feelings. Whether it is toward a pet, a family member, or an ideal, by holding the loved one in your heart consciously, even for 5 minutes at a time, and basking in the love you send them, you are programming yourself to experience that warmth and ease.

What does happen when you practice these things?[5]

- The neural pathways for peace of mind get stronger and more automatic

- Reduced worry, dread, and regret
- Increased self-empathy, patience, and compassion; feeling at ease
- Self-management instead of a feeling of being out of control
- Fewer errors and accidents that result from not paying attention
- Improved relationships and positive self expression
- Increased clarity and organization of thinking process
- Better problem solving
- Increased success—in your own terms—as a result of improved task management and attention to the details that matter *to you*
- Healthy curiosity
- Increased joy and gratitude
- Practicing delight instead of suffering

Exercise: How to Meditate (Simple do-it-yourself version)

1. Think of a tone that goes on and on, uninterrupted. Examples could be:
   - dial tone
   - jamming tone on a radio
   - note on a wind instrument
   - car horn
   - airplane

- chord on an organ or synthesizer
- for those old enough to remember, the tone signaling end of the broadcast day on TV
- constant soft sound of a steady rain

2. Whatever the tone, alter it in your mind (pitch, volume, quality) to one that is neutral or slightly pleasant.

3. Let it continue to play in your mind, uninterrupted.

4. Whenever you notice that your attention has wandered, for example, to an actual noise in your environment or to an itch on your arm, mentally acknowledge the wandering and return your attention to the tone.

5. Continue for 5, 10, 15, or 20 minutes. Initially, 5 minutes will seem a long time. As you practice, it will get easier.

6. Do this first thing in the morning and again later, in lieu of your afternoon coffee break.

7. Transition out *slowly*, allowing a full two minutes for your brainwaves to warm up to their normal pace.

8. Note: Setting a *pleasantly* toned alarm, like a chime, in advance as a timing reminder will help you keep from checking the time which would be another distraction.

What do I want to practice less?

RULE FOUR:

and furthermore...

Chapter Seven

PRACTICE GRATITUDE

There is always something to do.
There are hungry people to feed, naked people to clothe,
sick people to comfort and make well. And
while I don't expect you to save the world
I do think it's not asking too much for you to love
those with whom you sleep, share the happiness
of those whom you call friend, engage those among you
who are visionary and remove from your life
those who offer you depression, despair and disrespect.

—Nikki Giovanni

Pick a number. It can help to measure the subjective experience of personal growth.

You can define your *un*happiness by making a list of things that describe that condition and scoring them each on a misery scale 0-10, where 10 = totally unhappy. If you have trouble finding exactly the word that describes your feeling in this moment, check the Center for NonViolent Communication website. They have a thoroughly detailed list.

> www.CNVC.org

On a certain day you may see yourself as:

Sad	4
Cranky/irritable	9.5
Lost/lonely	8
Resentful	7

After a week or two of doing some work on yourself—reading, therapy, exercises, etc.—recheck those qualities and see if their numbers have shifted. The new numbers may indicate that you are marginally less miserable than you were before.

Sometimes one area may get worse before it gets better. It's called a 'healing crisis' that activates your immune system to do battle on your behalf.

Incremental change in a positive direction is exactly what you will want to achieve. Keep doing that and the numbers will help you notice the small but important shifts, the benefits of the many small positive steps you are taking. You will also be able to see areas that are more resistant to change and which may need specific attention or work.

> The only way to live
> is by accepting each minute as an unrepeatable miracle.
> —Jack Kornfield

Noticing That Life Doesn't Suck

Sometimes it may seem you have been working on yourself forever, and you're encountering more and more difficulties.

Consider this: in clearing an area of land for a garden, first you move boulders. That's tough heavy work and you may need help with that. Later you'll need to deal with some other big rocks, although they may be small enough to manage on your own, with effort—they are likely to be even more plentiful than the huge boulders. After that, there are even more, even smaller rocks.

It's helpful to keep in mind that at each stage the task is somewhat easier, your skill is more developed, and you *are* making progress, however long and arduous the undertaking feels.

GRATITUDE

The choice to be grateful is always available. How then does one stay here and do just this one thing? *Practice* is the simplest—and perhaps least helpful—answer. *Pay attention*, over and over again, is a little better. The over-and-over comes because attention naturally wanders, rather like a curious toddler. By choosing to be mindful—at least some of the time—we choose to gently take the toddler's hand and redirect it back to the chosen focus.

Here's something that you *can* do daily which may make a big difference:
Each morning, before you open your eyes and put on your day, think of three things for which you are grateful. Very small things count here, for example:

> *I am grateful for my blanket.*
> *I am grateful there is food in the fridge.*
> *I am grateful for my survival.*

Repeat this practice the last thing each night. These bracket your day with positive energy and loving acceptance of what is. Somehow it helps us find even more to be grateful for.

Pema Chödrön speaks of 'Cheerfulness Practice,' not as rah-rah as it sounds. Just the mindful effort to take situations we would otherwise grouse about, like traffic jams, and find in them small pleasures or curiosities rather than perceiving them as poor-me situations to get miffed about.

Keep a gratitude journal to help build this muscle. You can refer to this list for a lift when you feel down in the dumps.

A friend of mine gave me a book called *57 Reasons Not to Have a Nuclear War*, by Martin Asher and Lonny Sue Johnson (1984). It includes large and small things which are valued and appreciated in some way, from airports to chocolate cake to drive-in movies. Each time I pick it up I feel the gift of gratitude that there are so many things in the world worth saving.

When Pain Dissolves into Gratitude

Awake after a stressful dream in which I'd missed a flight, I sat, restless, in bed. My mind drifted away from the book in my hands. I became aware of a discomfort, almost a pain, a sadness in my chest.

Over the years of my work, both professional and personal, I've learned that, in lieu of resisting the sensations, I can honor the messages of the body, take time to give attention to whatever messages these waves of sensation might bring.

So I sat quietly with my eyes closed and dove into the feeling, not wallowing so much as letting myself sink into whatever information it might have for me.

A flicker of gratitude for the knowledge that this was possible, that I needn't run from pain, dismiss, deny, or bury it. The flicker, noticed, became a flame and then a wave itself, so strong it brought tears to my eyes as I was engulfed in joyful gratitude for the tools I have and capacity to use them.

Then came the urgent wish—prayer!—to capture the experience in words so as to share it. Again, the urgency and gratitude for what seems to me a most simple, convenient, and miraculous device: attention.

Exercise: A Practice of Gratitude
Settle into your breath without any goal. Take a few easy breaths, noticing any area of your body that is asking for attention. Feel free to shift or stretch if that would help you feel more comfortable.

After another breath or two, scan your body, as if you are taking a Xerox picture, from the roots of your hair to the soles of your feet.

Acknowledge any part that seems to have something to say, a message from your Feeler to your Thinker.

Does the tension around your eyes suggest you need more rest? Are your shoulders stiff from carrying the world in your backpack? Does your upper chest feel weighted down by all the *shoulds, musts,* and *have-tos*? Is there a worry knot in your midsection? Are your genitals demanding attention because they are tired of being ignored? Are your legs or arms loose and relaxed, or are they tightened to protect or spring away?

With this conscious awareness send a message of gratitude to the body for all the kindnesses that it has given you over your lifetime.

Think of specific physical joys in childhood. Feel the rush of the slide, the pleasure of running down a hill or playing in water. Of laughing deeply and uncontrollably. Of warming up with hot cocoa or cooling off with a popsicle.

Enjoy a few easy breaths as your body remembers.

Now, without effort, let that experience of joy expand, saturating every part of you and the space around you as you begin to glow.

With your next out-breath allow that glow to expand as a sense of appreciation and well-being to all the people you have loved, bathing them in this light.

Allow it to continue to grow to surround the Earth, picturing the planet's beating heart in synchrony with your own.

You can refresh this process whenever you like, especially if you are feeling down, by finding any moment of gratitude and letting the glow grow.

Where are the sources of Drama in my life?

RULE FIVE:

Drama
Is
Optional

Chapter Eight

DRAMA *IS* OPTIONAL

Think about the troubles you could avoid and the
stress you could eliminate if you made the *decision* to
ignore a light offense or a minor defamation,
or an unintentional snub—or even an intentional one.
Our reactions to the situation of our life are elective,
and *we* do the electing.

—Elaine St. James

Sometimes behaving dramatically is fun:
Dress-up parties, karaoke, touchdown spikes, or theatrical
performances. It can make something educational a whole
lot easier to take in. Drama is like spice: while a tiny bit,
thoughtfully placed, enhances the experience, an excess is
unpalatable.

Here in the material world, *drama is inevitable.*
There is illness, job loss, and heartbreak imposed on us.
These are called Primary Suffering.[6]

When I talk about Drama I'm really talking about
Secondary Suffering—that extended wallowing which comes
from the telling, re-telling, dwelling, attention-getting
externalization of emotions—which can contribute to our
belief that we've got it even worse than we actually do.

There is a choice we make—sometimes consciously—to
jump on the Drama Train with both feet and steam down
the track with little thought of who or what might be

damaged along the way. How many new cell phones have been purchased because the previous one was thrown in a fit of pique?

No such thing as "temper"

Thinking that *I have a temper*, as if it is something that exists separately from me and my choices, is an abdication of responsibility for behavior. The real issue is lack of self-awareness, self-management, and self soothing skills.

Here are my CHOICES:

Indulge My Drama-of-the Moment	OR	Change My Life
costs Keep Doing What I'm Doing Getting What I've Gotten		**costs** Takes Patience and Self-Control
benefits Brings Relief in the Moment		**benefits** Feel Better Later, Longer

An Evolutionary Benefit of the Limbic Hijack

When the deep limbic system is overactive it alters the mind's filters: what we are aware of and how we perceive it. High risk and time-pressured situations trigger the brain's survival mode. For the average person that means prefrontal cortex–Thinker–function is diminished, and survival mode is activated. We get tunnel vision and just these choices: fight, flight, freeze or submit.

A big jolt of adrenalin helps outrun the bad guys, if the terror doesn't take us down first. For highly trained first-responders, athletes, and warriors the neural pathways laid down by extensive training come into play, and the 'automatic' reaction is the one for which they've prepared. One police officer put it this way, "You don't rise to the occasion. You fall to the level of training."

Afterwards those athletes will still have a post-performance let-down as the adrenalin high leaves the system, but their rehearsals serve them *in lieu of the Thinker* that would be available in less emergency conditions.

When an overactive Feeler has gobbled up all your brain juice (glycogen) and you start calling your beloved some things that you'd fight someone else if they said that to her or him, you are in trouble. The loss of the cognitive manager–therapists call it *affect dysregulation*–can produce a kind of malignant entitlement where we behave in a way that is inconsistent with our highest values. We might victimize the partner, attack them from a poor-me stance, or use language as if we alone have needs. These are guaranteed strategies for losing the love you started with.

All **Life Is Suffering?**
The First Noble Truth in Buddhism says *All Life Is Suffering*. I translate that to All Life *Has* Suffering, a perhaps-noble way of saying 'Shit happens'. Can't really argue there.

The Second Noble Truth says *Suffering is caused by attachment*. To what? To things and people being how, what, where, and when we'd like them to be. To *shoulds* and *oughts* and *musts* and *if onlys*. Even our idea of love can sometimes be laden with 'if you really loved me you'd do this' or 'no wife of mine will do that' or 'what *will* I do if he/she doesn't call?' Recipes for Drama, no?

The alternative to this operatic suffering is a wildly radical concept that is sneaking into the western mind, the acceptance of What Is. Let me here celebrate the work of Byron Katie, *Loving What Is (2003)* and Tara Brach, *Radical Self-Acceptance: A Buddhist Guide to Freeing Yourself from Shame (2005)*. These are two wonderful teachers in the world of Radical Acceptance.

I don't suggest that we celebrate our disappointments. A simple and profound acceptance—that w*hat is simply is*—helps the mind move into position to address the present moment—instead of wasting our NOW time (and power) by begrudging the facts or longing for what 'should' have been.

Our initial disappointment when hopes are frustrated demonstrates that attachment to the hoped for scenario increases suffering—the deeper the attachment, the greater the suffering. Less attachment and we 'bounce back' more easily from the shortfall, getting back to practical matters like how to better the odds next time.

So when your honey stays out later than expected—as they may have done in the past—you can make alternative plans, perhaps including future discussions about this, while taking care of your right-now emotional well-being. Otherwise, we are merely longing for something that has already gone by.

None of this is to say that attaching is *wrong*;
it's inevitable. When our positive imaginings are fulfilled
just so, life is like an array of joyous sky rockets. Often,
though, reality falls short of our ideal scenarios and lets
us down, gently or harshly, and we suffer, a little or a lot.

So if I'm not 'wrong' to attach to a particular outcome, am
I 'right' to take life as it comes? I try to steer my clients
away from 'good,' 'bad,' 'right,' and 'wrong' because
using these judgmental words tends to shut down
communication. Using 'helpful', 'not helpful', 'useful',
and 'not useful', or simply stating one's preferences, gives
more opportunity to keep the conversation going.

As we learn to notice the ways we have *attached* to our
hopes we see how that sets us up when those hopes
are disappointed. We reduce suffering by peaceful
acceptance of what is—and thereby retain the energy in
the *now* to focus on whatever changes are still possible.

The Dance of the False Self
So much of the drama of our lives is in effort to maintain
the public face, dignity, and ego. A chance remark, taken
as insult, provokes defensive and attacking words. It is
no wonder that the old U.S. Department of War is now
called the Department of Defense!

My clients have shown me how strong this defensive
cloak can be, how thickly it distorts what was actually
said, and how ready the old scar tissue is to be awakened.
When we become able to hear with compassionate ears
instead of thick armor and sharpened weapons we can
listen past the clumsy efforts that others make.

Avoid *Co-miseration*

Sympathy is not equal to empathy. Commiseration can be validating if it lasts only a short time and provokes *empathy* as in "I can imagine how hard this is for you". But if it moves to "oh, yeah, me, too", *that* is sympathetic wallowing. It dumps more stuff BACK into your Container and may leave you feeling as bad or worse than when you started.

Whether you're talking about your noisy neighbor, a thoughtless spouse or the-contract-from-hell, getting a little off your chest—kind of like emotional flatulence —can be a relief, but when the room fills up with it, the atmosphere can become incendiary.

We wear the cloak of defense, the dress of ego, as a shield to help us pretend things we do not fully believe, perhaps this:

- I am whole

- I am capable

- I can manage my life

- I have intelligence

- I have it (mostly) together

- I am safe

- I am valuable, worthy

- I am lovable

- I am enough

When we address the shakiness of our core beliefs, then we crave fewer defenses because we can see that others' belief about us is just their belief, not who we are, and that we don't need their approval to be ok in ourselves.

On the level of the *Pseudo*-Adult, we fear what we do not yet know more than we embrace what we do. We sometimes believe more in our incapacity than we do in our ability to develop the skills and knowledge to thrive.

To give up—I like to say 'retire'—the *Pseudo*-Adult is to take ownership of both vulnerability and capacity, an act of deepest courage. The biggest risk is that of returning to pattern—almost inevitable—but at least temporary when we have committed to the practice of growth.

I'm a huge fan of the teaching poem 'Autobiography in Five Short Chapters' (see introduction) where the speaker takes us through the process of how change happens—confusion, denial, awareness, responsibility, choice, and perseverance, with relapse as an organic part of the process. When we feel stuck, it may be because we haven't yet appreciated the value of increased awareness of our current discomfort as an impetus to keep moving forward.

Overstating the Case Is One Way We Increase Unnecessary Drama

The more rigid a system is, the more vulnerable it is to collapse: flexibility and adaptability are signs of health. Do you limit yourself by using words that trap you in a less than ideal story about your reality? "Why can't you" asks for an explanation, from a negative position, when a simple request "could you?" might result in a positive response.

Language gives us a rich way to describe our experience and thank goodness for that! English itself is one of the richest, having a wider variety of choices than most other lexicons[7]. The sad thing is that we fall into habits and, instead of digging into the wealth of words available to us, use hyperbole and distort our own messages.

Hyperbole is the use of words of drama, exaggerated statements or claims not meant to be taken literally. We humans can use hyperbole to extend and intensify our stories so that others will have a sense of how we feel. We may behave as if exclamation points are the only kind of punctuation or use words like *millions* when what we really mean is *a whole lot*. We use *never* when we might more precisely say *seldom*. Our flair for the dramatic–and unconscious plea for sympathy–extends our suffering and invites others to share it with us. We use this luscious form of exaggeration so frequently that we periodically up the ante, invent more emphasizers, or even change the meanings/usage of words to help us underline and embolden how very, very, very much we mean it.

If these patterns appear regularly in your speech, notice if those words help trap your thinking, and whether they might derail your message by triggering resentment from others:

Ubiquitous Profanity is one sample–somehow if it's "effing cold" that's colder than just "cold". Like spices, a bit of colorful language can add zest. Too much dulls the palate.

Absolutes are words that often purport to cover more territory than is likely or even possible. Absolutes can exhaust us. We use them to make ourselves seem more injured and believe that things are worse than they may really be. If I say "everything went wrong this morning" what I mean may be that the alarm didn't work, I stubbed my toe, my gas tank was on empty, and I hit a bunch of red lights on the way to work. "Everything" is a rather large word for even that many calamities. To validate "everything" you would have to include at least World War VII and a broken fingernail.

Notice how you often you use these words.
See if a more moderate term would work better.

Absolutely

All, All the time

Always

Any, Anybody

Can't, Cannot

Constantly

Ever

Every

Everyone, Everybody

Everything

Just/Only

Never

Nobody, No One

Nothing

Only

Total

Whole, Entire

When used with precision, absolutes present no problem. For example, "I brought in *all* the groceries" claims that there were no groceries left in the car, which is easily testable, depending on the weather. However, when I say, "I *always* buy the groceries" and there is even one exception, like once when I was sick in bed, I have used the absolute word "always" hyperbolically. It then becomes a target for my partner who remembers another time and so it goes.

The absolute's lack of precision makes it the weakest point in an argument—and thus the most likely to be challenged—distracting both sides from the primary point, the trend which was exaggerated.

> Remind me of the human size of truth
> when*ever* I spout a big, ripe absolute.
> —Edward Field

Abandon These Tragically Inefficient Strategies

- Taking offense
- Righteous indignation
- Looking down from your high horse
- Mind reading
- Assuming
- Browbeating others to make your point
- Insisting on being 'right'
- Labeling others 'wrong'
- Attempting to manipulate by being pleasing

Notice the urge to defend. It is a pivot point, the *choice* point, where we may connect with another or push further away from that joy. Attachment to perceived insults or slights makes for an exhausting dance of ego and many lost opportunities for the deeper connections we seek.

Telling ourselves that others wish us ill, want to rank on us, or have an ax to grind programs us to listen for words or tones that can be taken to support that prejudgment. When we then–almost inevitably–hear something that we may perceive as evidence of the expected attack, it's usual to prepare to counter it without carefully verifying the intent or even evaluating how seriously that one statement or intention may need to be taken. We may simply stop hearing what is actually being said.

Respond, Don't React
Reaction comes, unthinking, from our most primitive survival instincts.

We think it's like this:

ACTION (the other's statement or behavior)
↓
REACTION

But it's really like this:

Beliefs held beforehand,
(usually as *should* statements)
↓
ACTION
↓
Self-talk (the story I tell myself, in light of the beliefs)
↓
Emotion
↓
Mindful RESPONSE *or* Thoughtless REACTION?

I think of *response* as a slower, more thoughtful process that engages the Thinker which is capable of considering outcomes, i.e. the likely results of one's words and actions.

Consider that the other's behavior reflects *them,* not you. Even if they *say* it's about you, it's merely their thought of the moment.

Try not to jump on others' errors. Take a breath or three. Use your Thinker-brain to be a loving witness to your Feeler's reaction by writing it down. *Write down* your reactions—instead of saying them or acting them out.

Avoid judging yourself or the other. Wait your turn to have a say.

Lead with acceptance and forgiveness and don't take missteps to heart. It will take a while to get good at this. You have your whole life. The effort is an act of love.

What Would Happen If I Met Each Perceived Insult with a Breath? Some space where it might sit there in the sunlight exposed, unadorned by my denials, rebuttals, or reciprocal ax-grinding? By letting it live in the air, naked in the echoing silence, unhidden by my noisy overreaction, I allow the source of the action or statement to be accountable without my stepping into a chastising parent role. I allow their humanity and responsibility to rise on its own.

Should that *not* happen, I am still left with options, among them:

1. to identify the action/statement and ask directly if the intention was as I perceived it

2. to state my own feelings and needs and request a *specific* behavior change

3. to determine whether further exposure to these behaviors is in my best interest now or in the long run

The decision to *inquire* from the place of generous curiosity rather than to *assume insult* can be a most lovely opportunity for the growth of intimacy. Meet resistance with love which dissolves the knots of anxiety, pain.

Does it require vulnerability, that is, a willingness to be in error? Ah, yes, but error is the easiest of thoughts. How bold and adventurous to say "Is this what you truly meant? Is this how you want us to be?" How rare and delicious might be the connections so built.

Learning Not to Scratch an Itch

When I was a child I had no idea that one could choose to *not* scratch a bug bite or poison ivy. It was inevitable that the smallpox vaccine itch and my chigger itch would marry and I'd have not one but two vaccine scars. Even later on, when I was 21, I had an allergic reaction to antibiotic treatment, and I dug into my palm with the nails of the opposite hand–the worst itch *ever*.

How is it different now that I'm older? One thing is that I've learned other options than scratching. Things like heat or cold, Benadryl cream, tea tree oil, or a baking soda poultice.

I've also learned that not every itch–literal or figurative –needs to be scratched. That urges are temporary, like feelings in general, and like the ocean's waves, rise, sweep across one, and fade back into nothing.

Resisting the urge to intervene makes one pointedly aware of those dueling ideas. "Do it!" "No, don't do it!" Whether we are talking itches or urges to make an ill-advised phone call or have that one-too-many drink, not responding to that primitive (relief!) urge to scratch requires the involvement of the grownup brain, the prefrontal cortex. The front parts of the mind can *pay attention*, notice the urge, and thoughtfully consider other options, surfing the urge, and watching it fade beyond memory.

These days, I can usually resist that urge to intervene which rises when I'm in a grocery store and I hear a parent's voice raised to a child. Although I confess that I may start a grownup conversation with the child which shifts the energy away from drama, for all three of us.

Being in the Moment: *Flow* as an Antidote to Stress
When we stop, breathe slowly and deeply, the mind becomes quiet enough to hear another level of truth. Perhaps it's the sound of the tongues of flame as they crackle in the fireplace, consuming log after log on a winter night. Perhaps it's the powerful wind making its last bid for domination and respect as winter days winnow down toward spring.

The voice of my small-child self may speak of excitement and anxiety about an upcoming event, or I may hear a habitual cautionary voice with my mother's critical tone and threats of dire consequences.

When I operate in automatic I miss the opportunity to screen for my *own* authenticity. If I do what I've "always" done I will get what I've always gotten.

Enter anguish with acceptance; dive in with love instead of armor. Instead of wringing yourself out, create one opportunity for true change.

Worry Is a Waste of the Gift of Imagination

Often people are troubled by their own thoughts, the awful it-might-happen stories they tell themselves, thoughts going around and around in their heads like gerbils on a wheel. With the exception of true disaster preparedness (for which, consult the American Red Cross), to run the movie of how terrible the future *might* be is to feel the catastrophe that may not come, to suffer *now* as if it is already happening. Some call it "awfulizing." In fact, if the worst *does* happen and you've worried yourself weak over it, you may well be *less* prepared to deal with struggles than if you had not thought about it at all.

What do all of these have in common?

HIGH EMO MUSIC (including some COUNTRY
    & most OPERA)
SUSPENSE or ACTION FILMS
HORROR MOVIES
INTENSE DRAMA
SOAP OPERAS/REALITY TV
SPECTATOR SPORTS
TELEVISION NEWS
THRILLER NOVELS
TRUE CRIME STORIES

Each of these sometimes *emphasize* drama and sensation. When deeply and emotionally involved in the shows we go through the emotions we might have if we were a participant in the event itself—as if it were our own real life. Such stimulation can even be addictive.

Have you noticed how much even commercials can get you going? Our unconscious minds don't discern reality from these entertainments, and these experiences trigger the biochemistry of stress and anxiety in an observer's brain and body.

When we practice powerless passivity in the face of perceived danger, we get very accomplished at experiencing anxiety without having a handle on it. The neural pathways for those activities and experiences then develop more solidly.

When visually stimulated by a *video* presentation (TV, film, and computer screen) those stressful memories record in a robust—and resounding—way. Vivid or disturbing dreams may be one result. Likewise, do pay attention to the music you are listening to and the emotions it evokes. What neural pathways are you activating with the stories in those anguished songs?

Effective Worrying

As difficult as it may seem, giving up worry over loved ones, even adult children, helps us recall that while preparation may be useful, *worry* is not.

Only worry with a pen in your hand—then it is called "planning." Better to list your concerns in great and glorious detail. Elaborate, extend the drama, dump all of it out on the page. Then attack the list planfully with "what ifs?" And "then whats?" What will I do if it happens *this* way instead of *that*?

Making *strategies* for dealing with whatever may happen, is a practical response to worries, as is discerning what parts of it are my business or none of my business. I love the expression "Not my monkey, not my circus" for these situations.

Triggers and Buttons

Unresolved experiences are like little sticks of dynamite. What may happen to set us off? What will push our buttons?

If we think of those trigger events as hitting a literal button on the outside of our Containers, we can imagine that it might be possible to map those buttons, label them, and, over time and with diligence, defuse their explosive potential.

Try this.

First, list what ticks you off. Write down the situations or events that set you on edge or get you grinding your teeth: angry thoughts or stress experienced in the body. (Actually this step alone can reduce angry acting out by safely *expressing* the emotion instead of stuffing it!)

Second, look for clusters, things on the list that have similar themes or patterns. Examples might include situations of perceived insult, time pressure, low blood sugar, a certain tone of voice, overt threat, word choice or pattern of speech. Sometimes we can be so afraid we will get triggered and totally lose our minds that we are rigid, hostile, and edgy most of the time. When you start sniping, ask yourself *what needs do I have that I'm not taking care of?*

The key in this analysis is to notice the *type* of situation that gets your goat—and has the power to up-end your mood.

Third, face the heavy lifting. Track that pattern back to its antecedents: a playground incident, having a partner who cheated, a lifetime of being called certain names, unfairness.

Fourth is *desensitizing* to delicately remove the wiring that ties the old experience to today's stimulus. The psychotherapeutic approach I use for this is EMDR (Eye-Movement Desensitization and Reprocessing).

Choose to Feel What You Feel: Steer toward Peace and Appreciation

To sit in silence simply feeling one's experience, communing with it, sending questions into it of *how* and *when* and *what*, is a conversation from which we may rediscover the center. The body will speak its feelings in *sensations* before they arise as emotions.

By learning the woof and warp, the underlying structure of the fabric of emotions, their color and shape, we may find the ability to alter them by the choice of attention, cooling a hot pain, focusing a diffuse discomfort, softening the blow of a sharp pain by going with it, like a martial artist.

By knowing the enemy, we become wise in its ways and may sometimes, disarm it.

Remember also that pain is a kind of energy. When it comes you can use it, direct it to somewhere useful. Live life to the fullest in any conditions but when the Drama Train goes by, just wave, and don't get on it. It goes nowhere, and fast.

Chapter Nine

HOW TO USE THE RULES

The only reason we don't open our hearts and
minds to other people is that they trigger confusion in us
that we don't feel brave enough or sane enough to deal with.
To the degree that we look clearly and compassionately
at ourselves, we feel confident and fearless about
looking into someone else's eyes.

—Pema Chödrön

Rule One: There is one and only one thing in the world
that we have power over and responsibility for–and that's
the person in the mirror. **Take responsibility for
yourself and your choices rather than focusing on
what others 'should' be doing differently.**

Rule Two: We are all Containers for feelings.
**Pay attention to how much you ask yourself to
hold, with self-care and support.**

Rule Three: Emotions do not mature. **Engage both
your Feeler and Thinker, in a mutually supportive
feedback arrangement, that continually redirects
you toward sustainable joy and compassionate
connection with self and others.**

Rule Four: What we practice we become. **Understand
that every repeated behavior lays down a track
for more of the same. Act from your very best self,
one moment at a time.**

Rule Five: Drama *is* optional. **Decide to use your attention to starve out habitual suffering. Take your life in the direction of the destinations that feed and celebrate your spirit.**

Lots of folks will tell you you're worth it. Test these ideas for yourself. Listen inside, to who you are and want to become. As you do that, offer gracious appreciation to *all* the versions of yourself. Each of us is a work in progress and merits that tenderness.

Enjoy the exploration and let me know what you discover.

Notes

1. "Parts is parts" refers to a commercial which derided unidentified, processed chicken parts.

   Information on Freud's *id, ego,* and *superego* can be found in Boundless (2016). *Boundless Psychology*
   https://www.boundless.com/psychology/textbooks/boundless-psychology-textbook/personality-16/psychodynamic-perspectives-on-personality-77/freudian-psychoanalytic-theory-of-personalty-304-12839/

   Discussion of *child, parent,* and *adult* parts is found in Berne, E. (2017). Transactional Analysis. Retrieved from
   http://www.ericberne.com/transactional-analysis/

   Internal Family Systems approach addresses a variety of internal personality parts and their functions. See Dick, C., Yalom, V., & Schwartz, R. (2009). *Instructor's manual for internal family systems therapy with Richard Schwartz, PhD.* Retrieved from
   http://www.psychotherapy.net/data/uploads /5113ce91c0a4d.pdf

   For a look inside the human brain, from a couple of different angles, see WETA (2017). Brain basics. Retrieved from
   http://www.brainline.org/multimedia/interactive_brain/the_human_ brain.html?gclid=CjoKEQiAuJXFBRDirIGnpZLEN4BEiQqVoKGol7 xiX2m4VtJWroHS3Cimsdw6mDz2V_9gwPQHjxdlYaArVk8P8HAQ

2. Maltz, M. (2016). *Psycho-cybernetics deluxe edition: The original text of the classic guide to a new life.* New York: TarcherPerigee.

3. Grossman, D. & Christensen, L. (2007). *On combat: The psychology and physiology of deadly conflict in war and in peace* (3rd ed.). Illinois: Warrior Science Publications.

4. The many benefits of meditation are discussed on the Transcendental Meditation website: www.tm.org. Other sources include Benson, Herbert, (1975). *The Relaxation Response,* New York: Harper Collins, as well as this Huffington Post article
   http://www.huffingtonpost.com/2014/09/19/meditation-benefits_ n_5842870.html

5. McGonigal, K. (2012). *The neuroscience of change: A compassion-based program for personal transformtion.* Sounds True audiobook.

   Baughn, E. B. (n.d.). [Review of the audiobook. *The neuroscience of change: A compassion-based program for personal transformation*]. CTAMFT. Retrieved from http://www.ctamft.org/ohana/website/?p=63905640

6. Vidyamala, B. & Penman, D. (2013). *You are not your pain:Using mindfulness to relieve pain, reduce stress, and restore well-being—An eight-week program.* New York: Flatiron Books.

7. Oxford University Press (2017). Does English have more words than any other language? Retrieved from
   https://en.oxforddictionaries.com/explore/does-english-have-most-words

elainebentleybaughn.wordpress.com/
blog: Toward a Drama-Free Life
facebook.com/EBBHomePage/

CPSIA information can be obtained
at www.ICGtesting.com
Printed in the USA
FFOW03n0542040717
37398FF